Social theory and education policy: the legacy of Karl Mannheim

INSTITUTE OF EDUCATION

University of London

Karl Mannheim Memorial Lecture

Social theory and education policy: the legacy of Karl Mannheim

Geoff Whitty

Karl Mannheim Professor of Sociology of Education

Extended version of a lecture
delivered at the Institute of Education,
University of London on 9 January 1997

First published in 1997 by the Institute of Education
University of London, 20 Bedford Way, London WC1H 0AL
Tel: 0171-580 1122. Fax: 0171-612 6126

Pursuing Excellence in Education

© Institute of Education University of London 1997

British Library Cataloguing in Publication Data:
a catalogue record for this publication is available
from the British Library

ISBN 0 85473-513-5

Typography and design by Joan Rose

Produced in Great Britain by Reprographic Services
Institute of Education University of London

Printed by Formara Limited
16 The Candlemakers, Temple Farm Industrial Estate
Southend on Sea, Essex SS2 5RX

I1-0012-GWKML-0797

Acknowledgements

I wish to acknowledge the assistance of the following people: Peter Aggleton, Cathy Bird, Jean Floud, Tony Green, John Hajnal, Stuart Hall, David Halpin, Alison Kirton, Yoshiyuki Kudomi, Robert Lawrence, Elizabeth Leo, Ian Lister, Peter Mortimore, Janet Ouston, Anne Peters, Miguel Pereyra, Stephen Pickles, Sally Power, Caroline Steenman-Clark, Sir William Taylor, and Patrick Whitty.

W.A.C. Stewart

As this lecture was going to press, we heard the sad news of the death on 23 April 1997 of W.A.C. Stewart, who had known Mannheim when he was at the Institute of Education and subsequently prepared his papers on the sociology of education for publication. My lecture is now published in his memory as well as that of Karl Mannheim. Campbell Stewart himself gave a public lecture on Mannheim at the Institute in May 1965 and my own lecture ends with some words taken from it.

Frontispiece photograph of Karl Mannheim in *From Karl Mannheim* edited by K.H. Wolff.

Karl Mannheim

Social theory and education policy: the legacy of Karl Mannheim

As members of the Academic Board we record our sorrow at the death of our beloved colleague Karl Mannheim. He came to us from another country after he had suffered persecution and many undeserved disappointments, We found in him a devoted scholar, a penetrating critic, and a warm-hearted friend. His profound reflections on the problems of human society had led him to a conviction of the importance of education and of the significance of our work in the Institute. We felt, therefore, that he came to us as a colleague and fellow worker, and not as a stranger. We are proud to think that he found a congenial home among us, and that he looked forward to his work with us with pleasure.

He held a Chair of Education in the Institute for only one year, but in that time he brought new inspiration to us and to our students, and he made great plans which we watched with interest and hope.

(Resolution of Academic Board,
Institute of Education, 16 January 1947)

Karl Mannheim was born into a middle-class Jewish family in Hungary at the end of the nineteenth century. He gained his Doctorate in philosophy in 1918 at the University of Budapest, after studying in Berlin, Paris, Freiburg and Heidelberg as well as Budapest itself. Significantly for his later career, he mixed freely in both positivist and anti-positivist circles. Nevertheless, he became most closely associated with the group that had gathered around George Lukacs, the Marxist literary critic who was briefly a Commissioner for Education in a short-lived Communist-Social Democratic coalition government. Although Mannheim declined to join the Communist Party,

Lukacs appointed him as a lecturer at the College of Education of the University of Budapest, which he later described in his curriculum vitae of August 1945 as Hungary's nearest equivalent to the Institute of Education.

As a result of his association with Lukacs, Mannheim fell foul of the new counter-revolutionary government in Budapest and left for Vienna in December 1919. From there, he moved to Germany and many of his most formative intellectual experiences took place in exile in Weimar Germany. He went initially to Freiburg and Berlin but settled in Heidelberg, where he was a member of the circle that had grown up around Max Weber and had continued to meet (under Alfred Weber) after his death in 1920. In 1930, Mannheim became Professor of Sociology and head of a newly created College of Sociology at the Goethe University of Frankfurt. In 1933, he was 'retired' by the Nazis from his position in Frankfurt and came, via Amsterdam, to England where he held a temporary lectureship in sociology at the London School of Economics. He also worked on a part-time basis at the Institute of Education between 1941 and 1945 until he took up a chair of education here on 1 January 1946. That was just a year before his untimely death at the age of 53 – exactly 50 years ago today.

My own life overlapped with Mannheim's by little over a week. This can hardly entitle me to claim membership of the same generation let alone the same 'generation unit' – to cite one of his concepts that has survived into the contemporary literature. So, apart from the fact that I now occupy the Karl Mannheim chair here at the Institute of Education, which was named in his honour, why have I chosen to give a professorial lecture on the fiftieth anniversary of his death and to take his work as a stimulus for a discussion of 'Social Theory and Education Policy'? My main justification is that, even though there have been major changes in the past 50 years, there are some striking continuities which suggest that parts of the legacy of Karl Mannheim are well worth holding onto.

The Institute of Education 50 years ago

In preparation for this lecture, I read a great deal about Mannheim's life and did a trawl of the Institute archives for material about the Institute in his time. A few things surprised me. As someone who has been complaining all year that academic work is being intensified, I was taken aback to discover that, just as we now teach EdD students at weekends, in those days they taught MA students on Saturdays (Clarke 1967:169). And, while the Institute was closed for nearly two weeks over Christmas this year, Karl Mannheim was apparently in his office on 27 December 1946.

On the other hand, some things remain the same. For example, one of Mannheim's last acts at the Institute was to write to the administration complaining about the lack of heating in that office (Woldring 1986:62). And our present Director and colleagues involved in teacher education will be particularly intrigued, and perhaps surprised, to know that one of the major preoccupations of Dr Jeffery, the then Director of the Institute, 50 years ago was how to keep members of His Majesty's Inspectorate at bay. In the very week of Mannheim's death, Jeffery had persuaded the Vice-Chancellor to send a letter to the Ministry of Education indicating that its attempt to insist on the right of inspection by His Majesty's Inspectors of work in the Institute and King's College would raise fundamental questions as to 'the de-limitation of the sphere of responsibility of the University' (6 January 1947). A few months later (4 June 1947), the Director advised the Vice-Chancellor that 'we ought to proceed . . . to defy the Ministry on this issue'. His grounds were subsequently stated in these terms:

> There can be no acceptance on the part of the University of any form of inspection of any School or Institution of the University that involves the presence of an Inspector [in his official capacity] at any lecture or tutorial class given or conducted by a teacher of the University in pursuance of his duty to the University. (Senate Paper, University of London, July 1947)

By threatening to abandon its plan to establish an Area Training Organisation (ATO) based on the Institute, the University was actually successful in facing down this threat, and was able to develop a collegial working relationship between the Institute and the Inspectorate in the years ahead.

Part of Jeffery's willingness to jeopardize the ATO and what he saw as the immediate interests of the Institute in the wider interests of academic freedom arose from his knowledge of the experience of Mannheim and other academic exiles from Nazi Germany. In a letter to Sir Ronald Adam at the British Council, Jeffery wrote:

> Some of us cannot forget that it was the beginning of the end in
> the German universities when representatives of the Party began
> to attend university lectures to see whether the lecturer was
> saying the right thing.
>
> (Jeffery to Sir Ronald Adam, 5 June 1947)

While this clearly has more than purely antiquarian interest in the context
of new threats to academic freedom in education, more directly relevant to
the central theme of my lecture today is a paper I came across in the wartime
archives by Jeffery's predecessor as Director of the Institute, the
distinguished educationist, Sir Fred Clarke.

Clarke had been impressed by his contact with Mannheim at meetings of
the Moot, a group of intellectuals that included such notables as J.H. Oldham,
Adolph Lowe, J. Middleton Murry, Sir Walter Moberly, A.D. Lindsay and T.S.
Eliot – a subject to which I shall return later in the lecture. In 1941 he therefore
arranged for Mannheim to teach classes at the Institute on a part-time basis
while he was still working at LSE. Negotiating this arrangement with LSE
was not straightforward, because of the strained relations between Mannheim
and the Professor of Sociology, Morris Ginsberg, and it was only secured
because of the close friendship between Clarke and the then Director of the
LSE, Professor A M Carr-Saunders (Kettler et al 1984; Woldring 1986) . For
two years, it involved Mannheim travelling between his home in Hampstead
to Nottingham, where the Institute was evacuated for much of the war, and
Cambridge, where the LSE was evacuated.

Then, as early as March 1943, Clarke was arguing the case for appointing
someone like Mannheim – and he clearly had Mannheim himself in mind – to
a new professorial position at the Institute as soon as the war was over. In a
note to the Delegacy responsible for the Institute, he wrote:

> The case for a professorship to work in terms of the sociological
> approach may be related to the uneasy awareness, now so
> widespread and yet so ill-defined, that great changes in the social
> order and the inter-play of social forces are already in progress –
> and that educational theory and educational policy that take no
> account of these will be not only blind but positively harmful.
>
> (Sir Fred Clarke, Director, Institute of Education, 18 March 1943)

In the event, Mannheim succeeded to Clarke's own chair in education, which on Clarke's retirement became separated from the Directorship of the Institute on the grounds that, while his successors as Director 'might well continue to carry the title and status of Professor [it was] too much to expect them to go on functioning in that capacity to any degree of effectiveness' – a claim refuted, of course, by more recent holders of the position. Although Mannheim's chair was in education, he took special responsibility for the sociological aspects of the field. His own conception of his post was a broad one influenced by his background and interests in philosophy, sociology and social psychology. He also approached it in much the same spirit as the *International Library of Sociology and Social Reconstruction*, which he founded and which reflected his conviction that sociology could provide the basis for a post-war social reconstruction in which education would play a vital role.

Mannheim for today?

I trust it is not just self-interest that leads me to the view that, fifty years on, the argument for having sociologists at the Institute is at least as strong as it was when Clarke was arguing the case. There is certainly a similar widespread sense today that significant but ill-defined changes in the nature of the social order are in progress. Not only sociology classes, but also the 'quality' press, Channel 4 and radio programmes like 'Start the Week', constantly debate the implications of living in post-modernity, post-industrial society, late capitalism, high modernity, post-traditional society or whatever. Chris Shilling, who favours the concept of 'high modernity', has written:

> Modernity brought with it a period of rapid change and the promise of control. In contrast, high modernity is a 'runaway world' which is apparently out of control . . . The consequences of high modernity . . . have the effect of introducing a radical doubt as to what precise goals education should achieve. These consequences also throw into question whether education systems have the capacity either to be fully controlled, or to accomplish planned social change with any degree of accuracy.
> (Shilling, 1993:108)

I want to suggest that, long before modernity was thought to have run its course, Mannheim was struggling with similar issues even though he responded to them in rather different terms. He once wrote that he wanted to learn 'the secret (even if it is infernal) of these new times', confronting problems that Kettler and Meja (1995) suggest, in the introduction to their most recent book on Mannheim, should remain 'irresistible to reflective people at the end of the twentieth century' (1995:1). Yet Mannheim barely gets a mention in the voluminous works of Shilling's mentor, Anthony Giddens, generally regarded as Britain's leading contemporary social theorist and, from this week, the new Director of the LSE. And, although Mannheim's work on the sociology of knowledge is still cited in other contemporary literature, as is his work on generation, Denis Lawton (1975) has quite rightly pointed to his relative neglect in education studies, even in the 1970s when his work on the social determination of ideas might have been expected to commend itself to the then 'new' sociologists of education. As far as the Institute of Education is concerned, Mannheim has been even less popular in the 1980s and 1990s. With only a few exceptions (e.g. Lander 1983), his work has not in recent years been seen as a major theoretical resource for research in the sociology of education at the Institute. Indeed, a month ago, not one of the 28 copies of the nine books by Mannheim held in the Institute library had been checked out on loan and even what is generally regarded as his most important work, *Ideology and Utopia* (Mannheim 1936), has been borrowed from the library only a handful of times since I read it as a Diploma student here in the early 1970s.

In some ways, this neglect is justified. It would, after all, be easy to exaggerate, not least for an occasion like this, the extent to which Mannheim is a contemporary thinker. Not only would this be in some tension with the thrust of his own writings on the sociology of knowledge, it would also involve doing a considerable degree of violence to his texts. To give but one example, I read with interest in an intellectual biography of Mannheim that he had written about the prevalence of 'an attitude of believing in nothing' and 'an endless craving for new sensations' (Loader 1985:189), statements that resonate with some contemporary characterisations of post-modernity. Yet when I traced this back to its source in *Diagnosis of Our Time*, I read:

> Whereas in some prominent individuals . . . falling into the abyss
> of the self without reaching the bottom presents itself as a
> grandiose struggle, a new Titanism, in the average man the very
> same dynamics lead to a frivolous attitude of believing in
> nothing and an endless craving for new sensations.
>
> (Mannheim 1943:108)

In both style and content, this sentiment places Mannheim in a very different age from our own, though even one of his own contemporaries, Professor Cavanagh of King's College, suggested that, perhaps because 'the German way of writing doesn't fit English', Mannheim's writings seemed 'to say little in a large number of obscure words' (Cavanagh to Clarke, 10 September 1942). Furthermore, the character of his work does not always make it easy for us to be clear what Mannheim is saying. Although one of his posthumous volumes was entitled *Systematic Sociology* (Mannheim 1957), Mannheim was hardly a systematic thinker. His work may be charitably considered what his intellectual biographer, Colin Loader (1985), euphemistically terms a 'dynamic totality', but even the books compiled during his lifetime under his own supervision are full of inconsistencies and repetitions.

Yet, for myself, in returning to Mannheim's work after an absence of 25 years, I do find it in some ways more pertinent than I did then. And, although circumstances are very different, his work as a whole deserves considerably more attention than it has recently received. As Meja and Kettler put it 'Mannheim confronts many contemporary sociologists with their hopes and misgivings, and offers them a model for resourceful thinking' (1993:xxxiv). Even some of the themes he addressed are surprisingly contemporary or at least relate to issues that continue to concern us, both in sociology and in education. His more theoretical work on the sociology of knowledge was unfashionable among Marxist sociologists of education in the 1970s partly because he resisted the notion that all ideas could be understood in terms of relations of class. But, notwithstanding the unremitting maleness of his language, one might have expected him to be cited more by feminist writers in the 1980s, since unusually among male sociologists of his era (and some would say since!) he had pointed out that women's interests were not best served by constantly having their voices mediated by men (Meja and Kettler 1993:xxxii). And, in so far as he generalized this argument to all social groups, it might be thought surprising that his work has not been recuperated in the 1980s and 1990s by contemporary writers who question the primacy not only of class relations, but even that of the 'holy trinity' of class, race and gender. Furthermore, his discussion of the growth of 'social techniques' which penetrate deep into our private lives and subject 'to public control psychological processes which were formerly considered as purely personal', in some ways anticipates Foucault's concern with 'moral technologies'. Finally, some of his discussions of consciousness and awareness anticipate contemporary notions of reflexivity.

Even so, it would be extremely difficult to characterize Mannheim as a post-structuralist or postmodernist theorist by any stretch of the imagination. His social psychology of personality was at odds with the notion of the decentered subject and the various 'solutions' he sought and provided to the 'problem' of relativism retain little currency today. His work was also firmly set in the redemptive project of the Enlightenment, albeit in the light of a recognition that it was in danger of all going horribly wrong. Thus, not only did his roots predispose him towards a 'grand narrative' approach to theory, his own solutions to a 'runaway world' were classically modernist ones. Kettler and Meja suggest that his 'project was to link thinking to emancipation – despite strong evidence against the connection'! (1995:1)

Nevertheless, like Mannheim, many contemporary social theorists still struggle with the prospect of losing any basis for claiming the superiority of one account over another – and continue to seek a viable epistemological basis for social science and even for social intervention. To put the problem in contemporary sociological jargon, rather than that of his own times, Mannheim sought a way of rejecting essentialism and foundationalism without being disempowered in the process. This has remained a recurring theme within social theory and in the sociology of education. Not only is it a major concern for those writers who still seek a basis for action in an uncertain world and in the light of postmodernist critiques of social science, it is also the very issue that I struggled with here as an MA student under Michael Young 25 years ago and which Young himself sought for a time to address through the social phenomenology of Merleau Ponty (Young 1973).

Subsequently, that particular Latin turn in the sociology of education was swiftly overshadowed by an Althusserian one and more recently by a Foucauldian one. However, other sociologists of education have tended to eschew that theoretical response to the cold climate facing them under Thatcherism in the 1980s in favour of a move into policy studies. For example, Brian Davies says of me, in his own inimitable way, that I have 'moved with some decorum, rather than any hint of "scramble" from being "new directions" first insider-critic to neo-Marxist curriculum analyst . . . to policy researcher and theorist' (Davies, 1994:14). In some ways, that move too was prefigured in Mannheim's own career. Jean Floud, who knew Mannheim in the 1930s and was later Reader in the Sociology of Education here at the Institute, suggests that by the 1940s Mannheim 'had turned from the fine points of the diagnosis [of the crisis] to the active political problem of controlling the descent into disaster' (Floud 1959:49). Put another way, the detached critical observer had 'grown into the political and social strategist who tries to understand so that others may be able to act' (Bramstedt and Gerth 1951: xii). And, in proposing 'Planning for Freedom' – a Third Way between a laissez-faire society and total regimentation (Mannheim 1951: xvii) – Mannheim went even further to suggest how they should act. With the hindsight of the late 1950s, Floud wrote dismissively of Mannheim's 'joyful conviction that Sociology, the science of social action, can banish or mitigate the horrors of social change' (Floud 1959:42). Although Mannheim's obituary in *The Times* claimed that he himself always insisted that he was concerned with diagnosis only, Campbell Stewart has suggested that his denial of partisanship was 'rather like Mr Roosevelt's claim to be neutral before Pearl Harbour' (Stewart 1967).

According to Yoshiyuki Kudomi, a Mannheimian scholar from Japan who worked with us here at the Institute last year, Mannheim certainly did not abandon the one project for the other (Kudomi 1996). Whether or not he actually made significant contributions to social theory after the mid-1930s, he continued to argue the need for sociological analysis alongside what he called 'social education' or the development of the techniques necessary for the creation of the democratic personality. He always regarded his prescriptions for policy in 'Planning for Freedom' as informed by his social theory even if that was not always clear to others.

Part of the reason why Floud and others could regard Mannheim's quest as irrelevant in the 1950s and beyond was that his diagnosis did not seem directly applicable to post-war social democracy. However, it is at least arguable that, after the experience of the past 17 years of deregulation and political hostility to planning, Mannheim's ideas about the damaging effects of atomisation and a *laissez-faire* society now have considerably more pertinence than they did then. In an interview with Kudomi in 1991, Campbell Stewart (who knew Mannheim and developed his writings on the sociology of education into a textbook (Mannheim and Stewart 1962)) mused about what Mannheim's reaction might have been to Mrs Thatcher's notion that 'there is no such thing as society' (*Woman's Own*, 31 October 1987). Similarly, Madeleine Arnot (in press) has suggested that it is salutory to re-read Mannheim in the current context of 'heightened individualism and atomism in society'. There would certainly be some poetic justice in Mannheim's ideas becoming relevant at the end of the Thatcher age, since his views were one of the main targets of F.A. Hayek's *Road to Serfdom*, which hurt him badly at the time of its publication in 1944 and which later became one of the key texts of the New Right revolution (Hayek 1944).

Social theory and contemporary education policy

As I said earlier, I would not want to push the argument for Mannheim's contemporary relevance too far. Indeed, I shall go on to suggest that his own prescriptions are of little direct help to us today. Nevertheless, I am inclined to agree with Colin Loader that 'if many of his answers can be rejected, the questions he raised . . . cannot' (Loader 1985:189). To illustrate this I will now shift my focus to the more conventional ground of professorial lectures here at the Institute and talk about some current work in my own field. In doing so, I will seek to show the importance of interrogating the 'common sense' not only of education policy but also educational research with the sort of lenses provided by social theory.

Today, just as in the days of Mannheim, too much education policy and a great deal of contemporary educational research has lost sight of Clarke's important insight that education policy needs to be informed by a sensitivity to the nature of the wider society. Mannheim himself was concerned about 'a tendency in democracies to discuss problems of organisation rather than ideas, techniques rather than aims' (1951:199). Yet, however implicated universities may now have become in the instrumental rationality of the state, if they are not to be the places to explore the relationship between education and the wider social order, it is difficult to see where that work will be done on a sustained and systematic basis. Although the production of knowledge increasingly takes place in a whole variety of sites (Gibbons et al 1994), there are some forms of knowledge production which are in danger of not taking place anywhere, since most of the other sites concerned with education are under even more pressure than we are to come up with 'quick-fix' solutions to immediate technical problems.

In what follows, I give two contemporary examples of where I think social theory can help broaden our understanding of the complexity of educational interventions and our appreciation of what is at stake. The first of these concerns the sociology of school knowledge, a field into which I was inducted in my time as a student at the Institute in the late 1960s and early 1970s, but to which I have returned recently in an empirical study of the implementation of cross-curricular themes, undertaken with Peter Aggleton and Gabrielle Rowe. My second example, which concerns devolution and choice in education, is drawn from the sociology of education policy on which I have been working for the past 15 years or so, mainly with Tony Edwards, John Fitz, Sharon Gewirtz and Sally Power.

Cross-curricular themes and the National Curriculum
One of Mannheim's observations was that academic teaching had contributed to 'the suppression . . . of . . . awareness'. Over-specialization had the effect of 'neutralizing the genuine interest in real problems and in the possible answers to them'. The student, he claimed, is 'rendered entirely uncritical by this method of teaching where everybody takes responsibility for a disconnected piece of [knowledge] only and is, therefore, never encouraged to think of situations as a whole' (Mannheim 1943:65-66).

This has been an enduring concern in English education and was something that Denis Gleeson and I wrote about in the 1970s when we argued the need for a 'meaningful and critical' form of social education (Gleeson and Whitty 1976). More recently, you will recall that, rather late in the day, Secretary of State Kenneth Baker introduced cross-curricular themes as an antidote to the subject domination of his National Curriculum, supposedly to help pupils prepare 'for the opportunities, responsibilities and experiences of adult life' (1988 Education Reform Act). The idea was that these themes would be taught mainly through the academic subjects using a permeation model.

Yet the research I undertook with Peter Aggleton and Gabrielle Rowe indicated that, while cross-curricular themes figured strongly in some very impressive and elaborate matrices being drawn up by senior management teams, the reality at classroom level was often very different. In practice, it was the subjects rather than the themes that were given prominence, as illustrated starkly by the following exchange which took place in a year 10 science lesson given by a senior teacher, who was also the school's coordinator for cross-curricular themes, and whose curriculum audit had indicated that science was a major context for health education:

Researcher: Shouldn't you write something about how people should clean their teeth?

Carl: I don't think we're supposed to do that.

Researcher: Why?

Carl: It's not what we're doing.

Researcher: Why are you doing this work then?

Carl: Because it's in the National Curriculum, I suppose *(laughs).*

Researcher: But the textbook has a picture of how you should brush your teeth.

Carl: I don't think that's really science.

(School G)

Now it would be easy to say that Carl had picked up the message emanating from government and teachers that cross-curricular themes were not important. And, to an extent, this is likely to have been the case, given the lack of priority given to the themes after 1990 by the National Curriculum

Council and the Office for Standards in Education. So it might seem that giving cross-curricular themes the same legislative basis as academic subjects would solve the problem. However, we also did a study in Northern Ireland, where National Curriculum planning began with the whole curriculum rather than individual subjects and where a set of similar cross-curricular themes was included in the relevant legislation. Their importance was also stressed in the Northern Ireland inspection framework and in teacher training. And, yes, all this did make a difference and the cross-curricular themes were somewhat more visible in classrooms in the province. But they were not that much more visible and the boundaries between subjects and between school and non-school knowledge still remained strong.

So how might we understand this? Here what we found helpful was not so much the work of of Mannheim himself, but that of my eminent predecessor, Basil Bernstein, the first holder of the Karl Mannheim chair. Although the roots of his own work derive more from Durkheim than Mannheim, his own attempts to develop social theory exemplify what Clarke seemed to be asking for from a Professor of Sociology of Education. They help us to see, for example, that much education policy misrecognises the nature of the relationship between school and society. Probably Bernstein's most quoted dictum is that:

'How a society selects, classifies, distributes, transmits and evaluates the educational knowledge it considers to be public, reflects both the distribution of power and the principles of social control.'

This requires that we locate the study of curriculum change in 'the larger question of the structure and changes in the structure of cultural transmissions' (Bernstein, 1971:47) . At the heart of his own theory is an attempt 'to explicate the process whereby a given distribution of power and principles of control are translated into specialized principles of communication differentially, and often unequally, distributed to social groups/classes' (Bernstein 1996:93).

In our own example of cross-curricular themes, Bernstein's work on the classification and framing of educational knowledge and his more recent writings on recognition and realization rules and vertical and horizontal discourses (Bernstein 1990, 1996) helped us to understand the formidable difficulties in switching between subjects and themes and, more importantly, what is at stake in doing so (Whitty et al 1994). As he himself puts it, 'attempts to change degrees of insulation reveal the power relations on which the classification is based and which it reproduces' (1996:21). Although the current debates about values in education and the community initiated by the School Curriculum and Assessment Authority perhaps go further towards recognizing what is at stake than the earlier publications of the National Curriculum Council, they seem equally naive about the extent to which schooling can compensate for society. Bernstein's work helps us to see that quick-fix solutions to enduring educational dilemmas, whether of a political or professional nature, are likely to have only limited impact and I would have to say that Mannheim himself might have learnt some useful lessons from his successor about this.

Devolution and choice in education

Not surprisingly, given the time at which he was writing, Mannheim favoured some forms of selection in education. But he also questioned the view that 'struggle and social competition always foster and select those who are the best according to an absolute standard of worth'. In doing so. he contrasted 'objective abilities' with 'social abilities' including 'pulling strings and discovering influential patrons' (Mannheim 1957:85). While not dismissing the importance of competition, he saw the dangers of its going too far and stressed the necessity of cooperation. He also contrasted what he called 'the new democratic personalism' with 'the atomised individualism of the laissez-faire period' and emphasized the need to break down 'the frustration of which comes from isolation, exaggerated privacy and sectarianism' and sought to mobilize instead 'the forces of group living in the service of a social ideal' (Mannheim 1945: 52).

In recent years, in this country and elsewhere, there have been concerted moves to dismantle centralized educational bureaucracies and create in their place devolved systems of schooling entailing significant degrees of institutional autonomy and a variety of forms of school-based management and administration. In many cases, these changes have been linked to an increased emphasis on parental choice and on competition between diversified and specialised forms of provision, thereby creating 'quasi-markets' in educational services (Le Grand and Bartlett 1993). Such policies received particular encouragement from New Right governments in Britain and the USA in the 1980s, and have subsequently been fostered by the IMF and the World Bank in Latin America and Eastern Europe (Arnove 1996).

Most advocates of choice and school autonomy base their support on claims that competition will enhance the efficiency and responsiveness of schools and thus increase their effectiveness. Many hope that market forces will overcome a levelling-down tendency which they ascribe to bureaucratic systems of mass education, while others see them as a way of giving disadvantaged children the sorts of opportunities hitherto available only to those who can afford to buy them through private schooling or their position in the housing market. Thus, advocates such as Terry Moe (1994) in the USA and Stephen Pollard (1995) over here have claimed that devolution and choice will be of particular benefit to the urban poor. Recently, even the political rhetoric of parties of the left has begun to place an increasing emphasis on diversity and choice in education.

Yet, my own reading of the evidence (Whitty 1997; Whitty et al 1997) suggests that there is little hope of such dreams being realized in the absence of broader policies that challenge deeper social and cultural inequalities. Although recent changes in modes of social solidarity may not be as momentous as terms like post-Fordism and post-modernity suggest, there does seem to have been an intensification of social differences and a celebration of them in a new rhetoric of legitimation. As the new discourse of choice, specialization and diversity replaces the previous one of common and comprehensive schooling, there is a growing body of evidence that, rather than benefiting the disadvantaged, the emphasis on parental choice and school autonomy is further disadvantaging those least able to compete in the market (Smith and Noble 1995; Gewirtz et al 1995: Lauder et al 1994). At the same time, it is increasing the differences between popular and less popular schools on a linear scale – reinforcing a vertical hierarchy of schooling types rather than producing the promised horizontal diversity. For most members of disadvantaged groups, as opposed to the few individuals who escape from schools at the bottom of the status hierarchy, the new arrangements seem to be just a more sophisticated way of reproducing traditional distinctions between different types of school and between the people who attend them.

It is too easy to accuse the perpetrators of such policies of bad faith. Even if there is some plausibility in the argument that handing decision-making down to schools and parents is a clever way of 'exporting the crisis', it is the misrecognition of the context that is more significant. As Amy Stuart Wells (1993a) points out, the economic metaphor that schools will improve once they behave more like private, profit-driven corporations and respond to the demands of 'consumers' ignores critical sociological issues that make the school consumption process extremely complex. Her own research in the USA suggests that escape from poor schools will not necessarily emerge from choice plans because 'the lack of power that some families experience is embedded in their social and economic lives' (Wells 1993b:48). Similarly, Gewirtz, Ball and Bowe (1992) suggest that, in the case of England, the new arrangements for school choice discriminate against those who have more pressing immediate concerns than being an educational 'consumer'. In their subsequent work (Ball et al 1996; Gewirtz, Ball and Bowe 1995), they draw upon the theories of French sociologist Pierre Bourdieu (Bourdieu and Passeron 1977; Bourdieu 1986) to explore 'the logic that informs the economy of cultural goods', which helps explain the class-related patterns of advantage and disadvantage they identify.

Through this work, and that of others, social theory is helping us to understand why, whatever the advocates of choice might believe, the provision of new choices to individual families is unlikely to overcome deep-rooted patterns of structural and cultural disadvantage. Indeed, policies that foster isolation, privacy and sectarianism are likely to obstruct rather than contribute to the achievement of that goal. Atomized decision-making in a highly stratified society may appear to give everyone equal opportunities, but transferring responsibility for decision-making from the public to the private sphere will reduce the possibility of collective action to improve the quality of education for all. That will only be achieved as part of a broader strategy of social and economic change, since Jean Anyon is probably right to argue that 'the only solution to educational resignation and failure in the inner city is the ultimate elimination of poverty and racial degradation' (Anyon 1995:89).

Social theory and educational research

Yet much educational research, as well as education policy, remains stubbornly decontextualized. My fellow sociologists have often been particularly critical of the currently fashionable work on school effectiveness and school improvement on this score. For example, the Australian Lawrence Angus criticizes it for failing 'to explore the relationship of specific practices to wider social and cultural constructions and political and economic interests' (Angus 1993:335). Thus, he says, the apparent message of some of the work 'that all children can succeed at school provided teachers have expectations, test them regularly, etc, shifts attention away from the nature of knowledge, the culture of schooling and, most importantly, the question of for whom and in whose interests schools are to be effective' (p.342). Richard Hatcher (1996) sees such work as downplaying the significance of social class, with similar consequences.

Certainly the more optimistic versions of work in this genre tend to exaggerate the extent to which local agency can challenge structural inequalities. Often it is not so much the specific claims, but rather the silences, that are significant. This is particularly interesting given that Clarke (1967:167) justified the appointment of Mannheim to the Institute partly on the grounds that 'English theorizing about education . . . tended to take for granted the actualities of society when it did not ignore them completely'. Even today, some of the school effectiveness and school improvement literature glosses over the fact that one conclusion to be drawn from a reading of the pioneering *Fifteen Thousand Hours* research (Rutter et al 1979) is that, if all schools performed as well as the best schools, the stratification of achievement by social class would be even more stark than it is now.

Angus also suggests that a lack of engagement with sociological theory can mean that such work is trapped in 'a logic of common sense which allows it . . . to be appropriated into the Right's hegemonic project' (Angus 1993:343). Thus, it sometimes seems that not only neo-liberal rhetoric, but also some forms of educational research, take the discursive repositioning of schools as autonomous self-improving agencies at its face value rather than recognizing that, in practice, the atomization of schooling too often merely allows advantaged schools to maximize their advantages. For those schools ill-placed to capitalize on their market position, the devolution of responsibility can lead to the devolution of blame.

In reality, though, many of the writers in this field do recognize such dangers. But Gerald Grace has pointed out that too often what Jenny Ozga (1990) terms the 'bigger picture' is not entirely ignored but alluded to in what he terms 'contextual rhetoric' at the beginning of a book or paper and then forgotten. The subsequent account may then still seem to exaggerate the degree to which and the circumstances in which individual schools and teachers can be empowered to buck the trends. It may thus raise unrealistic expectations which, when dashed, will only generate cynicism and low morale. For Grace, this makes such work an example of 'policy science', which excludes consideration of wider contextual relations 'by its sharply focused concern with the specifics of a particular set of policy initiatives . . . and is seductive in its concreteness, its apparently value-free and objective stance and its direct relation to action'. What risks being lost to view from this perspective is 'the examination of the politics and ideologies and interest groups of the policy making process; the making visible of internal contradictions within policy formulations, and the wider structuring and constraining effects of the social and economic relations within which policy making is taking place' (Grace, 1991:3). This requires what he terms 'policy scholarship'.

The sociological imagination

Yet I have always argued that it is not an 'either/or' issue. Good policy scholarship should subsume some of the more positive features of policy science but go beyond it – as is evident in Grace's own recent work on school leadership (Grace 1995). It seems unfortunate that, here at the Institute of Education, we have internationally renowned work in school effectiveness and in the sociology of education, but these groups rarely work together. Unless we constantly remind ourselves – and others – of both the possibilities and the limits of our mission to pursue educational excellence and social justice, we are liable to be misunderstood. Recently, an important critique of the OFSTED literacy study written by our own Peter Mortimore and Harvey Goldstein (Mortimore and Goldstein,1996) was attacked in the *Observer* by Melanie Phillips (Phillips, 1996). One of her arguments was that there was inconsistency between the claim that structural features of the three boroughs involved in the study helped explain the low levels of literacy of the pupils and other work emanating from the Institute that demonstrated that schools make a difference. It did not seem to occur to Ms Phillips that both could be true, which they are, but it does demonstrate the importance in all our work of constantly keeping in view the 'bigger picture'.

A graphic, though perhaps unfortunate, metaphor for the position I am arguing might be a 'vulture's eye view' of the world. Apparently a vulture is always able to keep the background landscape in view while enlarging its object of immediate interest. If anyone knows of a more cuddly creature that has a similar facility, I would appreciate hearing about it for future reference! Yet the analogy does not anyway quite capture the significance of the notion of the 'bigger picture'. The bigger picture is not just 'out there' in the background. As Giddens (1994b) says of globalization, it is not something that takes place beyond the local, it 'is an "in here" matter, which affects, or rather is dialectically related to, even the most intimate aspects of our lives' (Giddens 1994b: 95). With regard to education, Jean Floud (1977) pointed out some time ago that this idea is central to the work of Bernstein and Bourdieu in demonstrating, in their different ways, 'integral links, even homologies, between the wider social structure and educational institutions and processes' (Floud 1977:16). But, in another form, it was also there in Mannheim.

Making the sorts of connections I am arguing for here involves understanding the intersection between biography and history, between identity and structure and between personal troubles and public issues – what C. Wright Mills (1961) termed the exercise of the 'sociological imagination'. Mills himself can indirectly be considered a student of Mannheim through his contact with his supervisor and collaborator, Hans Gerth, who had been an assistant to Mannheim in Heidelberg before moving to the University of Wisconsin at Madison in the USA.

For Mills, the exercise of the sociological imagination was not a feature of the work of all sociologists nor was it necessarily restricted to signed-up members of that profession. But even in a context of supposed 'reflexive modernisation' (Beck et al 1994), I see little evidence of it being exercised liberally in contemporary institutional and political life. In these circumstances, I want to agree with Sir Fred Clarke's view that it is important for sociology to have a formal place in the study of education here at the Institute, if not with Mannheim's own more sociologically imperialist view that 'no educational activity or research is adequate in the present stage of consciousness unless it is conceived in terms of a sociology of education' (Mannheim and Stewart, 1962:159). Unlike Martyn Hammersley (1996) in a recent article, I do not believe that sociologists of education should be willing to accept the demise of their discipline on the grounds that something like Giddens' 'double hermeneutic' (Giddens 1984) has already taken a sociological way of thinking about the world into the commonsense of other educators and educational researchers. We have only to reflect on the examples I have given today to recognize that too often this is just not the case. Furthermore, in the light of current attacks on theory within initial teacher training and even within further professional development, Sir Fred Clarke's concerns may be even more pertinent than they were in the 1940s. Understanding the limits as well as the possibilities of action is an essential part of teachers' professional literacy, but we cannot be confident that it will emerge from the minimalist courses that are advocated by the present government and the Teacher Training Agency.

In the 1960s, Campbell Stewart (1967) commented that empirical sociologists of education had lost sight of the broader theoretical perspectives that thinkers like Mannheim brought to the subject. I am suggesting that this is more generally true of educational research today. But am I saying that any theory will do? Clearly, I have emphasized here theories that challenge a 'new common sense' in education policy and in research that celebrates and exaggerates the extent to which all individuals and institutions have a realistic chance to grasp their own futures. Some other theories serve to bolster that commonsense and, in doing so, help to legitimate and maintain existing relations of power. My own preference is for theories that provide a different set of lenses from those we take-for-granted. Yet we also need to recognize, like Mannheim, that those perspectives that give us a different 'take' on reality in one era can become part of the taken-for-grantedness of another. To that extent, there are some attractions in Stephen Ball's advocacy of the 'semiotic guerrilla warfare' of poststructuralist and deconstructionist views of the role of theory (Ball 1995). However, like Mannheim, I am still committed to a version of the 'modernist' project in social research, though hopefully somewhat more reflexive about its own limits and possibilities than he was in his later years. But in interrogating theory with data and vice versa, I do want to claim that some theories are more powerful than others in helping us to see what is at stake in education and the limits and possibilities of professional and political interventions.

For example, it seems to me that those versions of post-modernism that positively celebrate 'difference' and 'heterogeneity' serve to legitimate the rhetoric of reform, while those which emphasise 'distinction' and 'hierarchy' within a fragmented social order (Lash 1990) provide a more adequate theorization of its reality. Indeed, I myself would go further and argue, along with David Harvey (1989), that to regard the current espousal of heterogeneity, pluralism and local narratives as indicative of a new social order may be to mistake phenomenal forms for structural relations. In other words, postmodernist cultural forms and more flexible modes of capital accumulation may themselves be shifts in surface appearance, rather than signs of the emergence of some entirely new post-capitalist or even post-industrial society. To make policy on a different assumption may well be positively harmful.

Yet I do recognize that such a perspective could all too easily lead to inaction rather than action. There have long been those who have seen some forms of sociological theorizing about education as generating total pessimism about the chances of things being different and thereby stripping teachers of any sense of agency. In that sense, the sort of social theory I am talking about could be seen to feed a Gramscian 'pessimism of the intellect'. Indeed, I heard Gerald Grace (1996) make a similar point recently. Significantly, though, he went on to emphasise that policy scholarship would help to generate 'complex hope' rather than the 'simple hope' of the school improvement lobby – and thereby presumably justify a *more realistic* degree of optimism of the will.

Education policy and democratic planning

However, it might be argued that, although Grace's own notion of 'policy scholarship' is informed by a sense of both theory and history which helps us to recognize the 'bigger picture' within which educational policy and practice is located, the term itself reflects too much of a disarticulation between the concerns of the academy and those of the world beyond. Therefore I now want to consider whether there is any role for social theorists to move beyond diagnosis to prescription about possible interventions. Jean Floud (1959) has implied that Mannheim would have done better to continue 'to try to understand and diagnose, rather than to plan and legislate' (Floud 1959:62). Although she had admired Mannheim when a student at LSE and subsequently assisted him with his researches, Floud (1959) came to regard not only his view of the power of social science as suspect, but also his view of democracy. Following A D Lindsay, she claimed that, within a decade of his death, it was universally recognized that 'Mannheim's "planning for democracy" . . . was not "democratic planning"; and people were beginning to think in any case that "democratic planning" was a contradiction in terms . . . ' (Floud 1977:8). But it does not seem to me that it is *necessarily* a contradiction in terms and nor do I think we should eschew the task of considering how the rhetoric and reality of education might be brought into closer correspondence. However, I would no longer argue, even if I once did, that there is an imperative that requires all social theorists to make such a move.

Mannheim is probably best known for his idea of free-floating or socially unattached intellectuals. In the 1970s, sociologists of education often preferred to see themselves as the Gramscian organic intellectuals of the working class. Indeed, it embarrasses me to have to confess on this particular occasion that, in an interview I gave in America quite recently, I said that I would rather be the Antonio Gramsci Professor of Sociology of Education than the Karl Mannheim one! But, increasingly, other sociologists have reconstituted themselves as Foucauldian specific intellectuals as the notion of a 'movement' to engage with has become difficult to sustain. Yet, while sociology of education seems to have become more isolated in the academy and somewhat disengaged from wider social movements, grander theorists such as Anthony Giddens seem to be taking social theory back to its wider concerns and showing a willingness to try to address the political challenges posed by a changing social order. Giddens notes that 'on each side of the political spectrum today we see a fear of social disintegration and a call for a revival of community', but argues himself for the development of a 'dialogic democracy' in keeping with his analysis of the nature of the age and its attendant dangers (Giddens 1994a:124). Though he may not recognize it, this is a truly Mannheimian project, albeit one shorn of its confidence and certainty. In this contemporary form, it could now usefully be carried into thinking about education policy.

However, we should also recognize that it is not only sociology of education that has become disarticulated from its object of study or engagement. Using Bourdieu's notion of social field, Jim Ladwig (1994) argues that the field of education policy itself in the USA has developed a considerable degree of autonomy. He observes that the very fact that observations about the 'failure' of education policy or its implications for particular groups pose no threat to the relatively autonomous field of education policy is indicative of the extent to which education policy as a field has become self-justifying and self-perpetuating. The way in which the present UK government declares policies a success and extends them even before they have been evaluated, and sometimes even before they have been implemented, is another example of this.

Unfortunately, though, Mannheim's own prescriptions do not provide us with a good model for rearticulating social theory with education policy and both with educational practice. For example, in his later writings advocating a revitalized conception of citzenship fostered through education for democracy, he seemed to forget some of the complexity of his earlier sociological work on generation units. Hoyle (1962) subsequently questioned how far Mannheim's consensual approach to social integration was feasible even in his own day and the increasing diversity of contemporary societies certainly makes his rather uni-dimensional proposals seem even more simplistic and problematic today.

Nevertheless, it should already be obvious from what I have said that I still regard social theory as potentially relevant to educational policy and practice, at least in so far as it can help to make sense of the broader context of educational reform and demonstrate its utter complexity – even if it cannot prescribe action. This has some parallels with the view Mannheim expressed in *Ideology and Utopia,* where he wrote of political sociology that 'it must teach what alone is teachable, namely, structural relationships; the judgements themselves cannot be taught but we can become more or less adequately aware of them and we can interpret them' (Mannheim 1936: 146).

Mannheim and the Moot

In my book *Sociology and School Knowledge*, I argued that 'one of the things that sociologists would almost certainly bring to such discussions [about policy and practice] would be a degree of caution, derived partly from . . . the study of past attempts at innovation' (Whitty 1985:176). However, I also suggested that 'the practical implications of [sociological] work for . . . political and educational practice [are] as much concerned with the ways in which policy is made as with specific substantive policies' (Whitty 1985:82). Some people have suggested to me that the fiftieth anniversary of Mannheim's death might be an appropriate time to revive something like the wartime Moot in which Mannheim developed his ideas on planning and democracy. The Moot brought together a group of distinguished Christian laypeople and clergy with leading intellectuals, both Christian and non-Christian, at a series of residential weekends between 1938 and 1947 which came to focus on the post-war social and political reconstruction. It has been seen as an early think-tank, although in a fascinating recent paper about the Moot, Sir William Taylor (1996) suggests that, rather like the All Souls Group with which it overlapped, it was closer to the model of a dining club or discussion group than a direct disseminator of policy proposals. Nevertheless, Mannheim became a key member – arguably the key member – of this particular group, as did Sir Fred Clarke, who took it upon himself to tease out the educational implications of Mannheim's general prescriptions about 'Planning for Freedom'. As a result, some of Mannheim's ideas can be thought to have indirectly influenced the1944 Education Act (Clarke 1967:166).

Taylor suggests that 'democracy benefits when politicians, academics, administrators and professionals have opportunities to engage in policy debate away from their desks and in a context that requires neither agreed conclusions nor clear decisions'. He also says 'the ability of these informal groups to influence policy depends almost entirely on who they are able to attract as members'. Yet it seems to me that, for this day and age, groups like the wartime Moot and even the All Souls Group operate with an exclusive and rather patronizing view of democracy. Even if Stewart (1967) and Loader (1985) may have been right to claim that critics such as Hoyle (1962, 1964) overstated the extent of Mannheim's elitism, the changes that have subsequently taken place in society now demand more radical conceptions of democracy – and they also demand more open discussion of what those alternatives might be. We still need to move beyond the 'old' politics of education and open up deliberation and decision-making to excluded constituencies. Thatcherism in education, as elsewhere, was partly successful because whole constituencies felt excluded from the social democratic settlement of the post-war era. Indeed, it appealed to them over the heads of 'bureau-professionals' who were characterized as having got fat by controlling people's lives in the name of rationality and progress. Through its policies of 'devolution', Mrs Thatcher's government was able to characterize itself as democratic and the liberal educational establishment as elitist and engaged in restrictive practices behind closed doors.

Not that Thatcherism has actually established 'deep democracy'. Within education, decisions have come to be made by groups that are even less democratically rooted than those they have replaced. Whatever the rhetoric of devolution may suggest, it is quite clear that significant constituencies have remained excluded from education policy and decision-making either intentionally or, just as often, as an unintended consequence of decisions made with the best of intentions. The result, as I implied earlier, is that recent market-oriented reforms are encouraging advantaged schools and advantaged families to enhance their advantage (Whitty 1997). This suggests that, if equity and social cohesion are to remain important considerations within education policy, there is an urgent need to balance consumer rights with a new conception of citizen rights to give voice to those excluded from the benefits of both social democratic and neo-liberal policies.

Yet, in so far as social relations are becoming increasingly accommodated in the notion of the strong state and the free economy (Gamble 1988), neither the state nor civil society is currently much of a context for active democratic citizenship through which social justice can be pursued. The reassertion of citizenship rights in education would seem to require the development of a new public sphere somehow between the state and a marketized civil society, in which new forms of collective association can be developed. Foucault – a social theorist whose work some people will be surprised to hear me cite – pointed out that what he called new forms of association, such as trade unions and political parties, arose in the nineteenth century as a counter-balance to the prerogative of the state, and that they acted as the seedbed of new ideas (Foucault 1988). We need to consider what might be the contemporary versions of these collectivist forms of association to counterbalance not only the prerogative of the state, but also the prerogative of the market. Part of the challenge must be to move away from atomised decision-making to the reassertion of collective responsibility for education – but without recreating the sort of overcentralized planning favoured by Mannheim and whose shortcomings have helped to legitimate the current tendency to treat education as a private good rather than a public responsibility.

Beyond the Moot

If new approaches to collective decision-making are to be granted more legitimacy than previous ones, careful consideration will need to be given to the composition, nature and powers of new institutional forms if they are to prove an appropriate way of reasserting democratic citizenship rights in education in the late twentieth century and beyond. They will certainly need to respond to critiques of conventional forms of political association in most modern societies. While market forms are part of a social text that helps to create new subject positions which undermine traditional forms of collectivism, those forms of collectivism themselves often failed to empower many members of society, including women and minority ethnic groups.

In seeking to avoid the atomization of educational decision-making, and associated tendencies towards fragmentation and polarization between schools and within schools, we need to create new collective contexts within civil society for determining institutional and curricular arrangements that are genuinely inclusive. These will need to reflect a conception of citizenship that entails creating unity without denying specificity (Mouffe 1989). Arguably, having a National Curriculum and devolved decision-making does at least recognize both parts of this requirement, but we have to find more adequate ways of doing so. Some of the discussions at the Moot about structures and values remain of interest in this connection, but such difficult public issues now need to be confronted publicly rather than in private.

In this context, current forms of democracy in England may be even less appropriate than those associated with directly elected School Boards in the nineteenth century, which used 'an advanced form of proportional representation [which] ensured that all the major political and religious groupings could be represented on the School Boards, so that positive policies at this level achieved a genuine consensus' (Simon 1994:12). We now have to ask what are the appropriate constituencies and forms of democracy through which to express the complexities of communities in the late twentieth century.

To date, the Left has done little to develop an approach to public education which looks significantly different from the state education so often criticized in the past for its role in reproducing and legitimating social inequalities (Young and Whitty 1977). Even if the social democratic era looks better in retrospect, and in comparison with current policies, than it did at the time, that does not remove the need to rethink what might be progressive policies for the next century. If we do not take the opportunity to do this, we may even find the policy agenda dominated by those radical rightist commentators who will foster the very forms of individualism and competition that Mannheim saw as such a threat to the future of liberal democracies.

This might involve moving still further towards marketized and even privatized forms of education provision. Indeed, some advocates of market forces have argued that the indifferent performance of the reforms to date is merely evidence that they have not gone far enough. James Tooley (1995), for example, favours an even more deregulated system and the abandonment of a centrally prescribed curriculum. He also claims that the potential of markets in education cannot be properly assessed by looking at the effects of quasi-markets or what he prefers to term 'so-called' markets. He is right, of course, to remind us of the equity failings of democratic systems, but as Smith and Meier (1995) point out in response to Chubb and Moe (1990), the failings of existing forms of democratic governance may necessitate reforming them rather than abandoning them.

Regrettably, our recent fascination with recent neo-liberal reforms may have blinded us to the potential of other ways of struggling to improve the education of disadvantaged groups. As James Henig rightly says of a similar situation in the USA, 'the sad irony of the current education-reform movement is that, through over-identification with school-choice proposals rooted in market-based ideas, the healthy impulse to consider radical reforms to address social problems may be channeled into initiatives that further erode the potential for collective deliberation and collective response' (Henig 1994:222).

If as a society we are thus in danger of being captured – or even trapped – by the discourse of marketization (Bowe, Ball, and Gewirtz 1994), social theorists may even have a role in pointing to other possibilities. Indeed, it may be time to try to develop what Erik Olin Wright (1995) terms 'real utopias'. Wright works at the University of Wisconsin in Madison, which coincidentally is one of the American universities to which Mannheim himself nearly went rather than coming to London and also one with which I myself have developed close links. Wright takes the view that 'what is pragmatically possible is not fixed independently of our imaginations, but itself shaped by our visions'. His own Real Utopias Project works through 'utopian ideals that are grounded in the real potentials of humanity', but also with 'utopian destinations that have accessible waystations' and 'utopian designs of institutions which can inform our practical tasks of muddling through in a world of imperfect conditions for social change' (p.ix). Even though Mannheim was suspicious of many forms of utopianism and said, in *Man and Society in an Age of Reconstruction*, that '"Planning" is not utopian; [because] it accepts the historically determined present state of society as its datum' (Mannheim, 1940), this formulation itself suggests that he might not have been averse to Wright's notion of 'real' utopias.

There is currently a great deal of discussion about ways of democratizing the state and civil society short of major constitutional changes. Mike Geddes (1996), for example, sees the future in terms of attempts to combine the virtues of different approaches to democracy. In particular, he seems to favour combining elements of representative and participatory democracy, by such devices as decentralizing the policy process and establishing community councils, citizens' juries, and opinion panels. However, in view of the lack of a firm constitutional basis for most such innovations, they tend to create ambiguity about whether they constitute democratic involvement in decision-making or mere consultation. Nevertheless, they may act as seedbeds for new ideas about democratic governance and contexts for Gramscian prefigurement struggles. Similarly, in the USA, Joshua Cohen and Joel Rogers (1995) take the view that it is possible to improve the practical approximation, even of market societies, to egalitarian democratic norms. They argue that, by altering the status of 'secondary associations' within civil society, associative democracy can 'improve economic performance and government efficiency and advance egalitatian-democratic norms of popular sovereignty, political equality, distributive equity and civic consciousness' (p.9).

I hope we can now develop new democratic forums in which to examine such ideas further and their implications for education policymaking. But rather than explore them in the sort of context in which Mannheim tried out his own ideas, we need to develop a more democratized version of the Moot – perhaps employing the new media. It may even be that the Internet has a role to play here, though I am by no means convinced that it is by definition a democratic medium and we would need to be as alert as Mannheim was in the case of other media to its totalizing and totalitarian possibilities (Mannheim 1943:2).

Concluding remarks

When one of my colleagues first heard that I was giving this lecture, she asked me whether Mannheim was still alive. Someone else misread my headed notepaper which says 'Karl Mannheim Professor of Sociology of Education' and asked me how I found it having someone so famous in my department! I hope I have shown that, although he has in fact been dead for 50 years, there are aspects of Mannheim's project that are worth keeping alive.

Indeed, I think much of the project which Mannheim outlined in the curriculum vitae he submitted to Sir Fred Clarke and which Clarke, in turn, submitted to the Registrar of the University of London in August 1945, is still worthy of pursuit:

    a)   To establish Sociology both as a theoretical and empirical study and develop research methods in these fields.

    b)   To study the philosophical and sociological foundations of education and the educative significance of social institutions.

c) To achieve a deeper understanding of the contemporary social and cultural crisis and to investigate the prospects of social education.

(Curriculum vitae accompanying a letter from Clarke to the Registrar, University of London, 24 August 1945)

Perhaps, though, I could be permitted to add a fourth element which builds upon but goes beyond Mannheim's own work with the Moot:

d) To explore new ways of democratizing education policy-making.

As Sir Fred Clarke said in concluding his own memoir of Mannheim, 'the best tribute we can pay to him is to follow up and develop the inspiration he gave and, if we can do so, to find and equip those who may be able, however haltingly, to walk in his ways' (Clarke 1967: 169). For, in the words with which Campbell Stewart (1967) concluded what was probably the last public lecture given on Mannheim here at the Institute, 'before long we shall need again to call on the kind of perspective which Karl Mannheim could command and which for the moment we seem to be too committed [to other priorities] to realize we have lost' (p37).

Note

A shorter version of this lecture was published in the *British Journal of Sociology of Education*, 18(2), 1997.

References

Angus, L. (1993), 'The Sociology of School Effectiveness', *British Journal of Sociology of Education*, 14(3):333-345.

Anyon, J. (1995), 'Race, Social Class, and Educational Reform in an Inner-city School', *Teachers College Record*, 97(1):69-94.

Arnot, M.(in press), '"Distressed Worlds": Social injustice through educational transformations' in D. Carlson and M. W. Apple (eds) *Critical Educational Theory in Unsettling Times*, Boulder, Westview Press.

Arnove, R. (1996), 'Neo-Liberal Education Policies in Latin America: Arguments in Favor and Against'. Paper delivered to the Comparative and International Education Society, Williamsburg, March 6-10.

Ball, S. J. (1995), 'Intellectuals or Technicians? The Urgent Role of Theory in Educational Studies', British Journal of Educational Studies, 43(3):255-271.

Ball, S.J., Bowe, R. and Gewirtz, S. (1996), 'School choice, social class and distinction: the realization of social advantage in education', *Journal of Education Policy,* 11(1):89-112.

Beck, U., Giddens, A. and Lash, S. (1994), *Reflexive Modernization*, Cambridge, Polity Press.

Bernstein, B. (1971), 'On the Classification and Framing of Educational Knowledge' in M. F. D. Young (ed.), *Knowledge and Control*, London, Collier Macmillan.

—   (1990), *The Structuring of Pedagogic Discourse*, London, Routledge.

—   (1996), *Pedagogy, Symbolic Control and Identity*, London, Taylor & Francis.

Bourdieu, P. (1986), *Distinction, a social critique of the judgement of taste.* London, Routledge.

Bourdieu, P. and Passeron, J.P. (1977), *Reproduction in Education, Culture and Society*, London, Sage.

Bowe, R., Ball, S. J., and Gewirtz, S. (1994), 'Captured by the Discourse: issues and concerns in researching parental choice', *British Journal of Sociology of Education*, 15(1):63-78.

Bramstedt, E. K. and Gerth, H. (1951), 'A Note on the Work of Karl Mannheim' in K. Mannheim, *Freedom, Power and Democratic Planning*, London, Routledge.

Chubb, J. and Moe, T. (1990), *Politics, Markets and America's Schools*, Washington, Brookings Institution.

Clarke, F. (1967), 'Karl Mannheim at the Institute of Education', Appendix B of F W Mitchell, *Sir Fred Clarke: Master-Teacher 1880-1952*, London, Longmans.

Cohen, J. and Rogers, J. (1995), *Associations and Democracy*, London, Verso.

Davies, B. (1994), 'Durkheim and the Sociology of Education in Britain', *British Journal of Sociology of Education*, 15(1):3-25.

Floud, J. (1959), 'Karl Mannheim' in A. V. Judges (ed), *The Function of Teaching,* London, Faber & Faber.

—   (1977), *Functions, Purposes and Powers in Education*, The Charles Gittins Memorial Lecture, Swansea, University College of Swansea.

Foucault, M. (1988), *Politics/Philosophy/Culture*, ed. L. D. Kritzman, New York, Routledge.

Gamble, A. (1988), *The Strong State and the Free Economy*, London, Macmillan.

Geddes, M. (1996), *Extending Democratic Practice in Local Government*, Greenwich, Campaign for Local Democracy.

Gewirtz, S., Ball, S. J. and Bowe, R. (1992), 'Parents, privilege and the Educational Marketplace'. Paper present at the annual conference of the British Educational Research Association, Stirling, 31 August.

—   (1995), *Markets, Choice and Equity*, Buckingham, Open University Press.

Gibbons, M., Limoges, C., Nowotny, H., Schwartzman, S., Scott, P. and Trow, M. (1994), *The New Production of Knowledge*, London, Sage.

Giddens, A. (1984), *The Constitution of Society*, Cambridge, Polity Press.

—   (1994a), *Beyond Left and Right: The Future of Radical Politics*, Cambridge, Polity Press.

_   (1994b), 'Living in a Post-Traditional Society' in U. Beck et al, *Reflexive Modernization*, Cambridge, Polity Press.

Gleeson, D. and Whitty, G. (1976), *Developments in Social Studies Teaching*, London, Open Books.

Grace, G. (1991), 'Welfare Labourism versus the New Right', *International Studies in Sociology of Education*, 1(1):25-42.

—   (1995), *School Leadership: Beyond Education Management: an essay in policy scholarship*, London, Falmer Press.

—   (1996), 'Urban Education and the Culture of Contentment'. Lecture given at King's College London, 3 December.

Hammersley, M. (1996), 'Post Mortem or Post Modern? Some Reflections on British Sociology of Education', *British Journal of Educational Studies*, 44(4):394-406.

Harvey, D. (1989), *The condition of postmodernity: an enquiry into the origins of cultural change*, Oxford, Basil Blackwell.

Hatcher, R. (1996), 'The limitations of the new social democratic agenda' in R. Hatcher and K. Jones (eds) *Education after the Conservatives*, Stoke-on-Trent, Trentham Books.

Hayek, F. A. (1944), *The Road to Serfdom*, London, Routledge.

Henig, J. R. (1994), *Rethinking School Choice: Limits of the Market Metaphor*, Princeton, Princeton University Press.

Hoyle, E. (1962), 'Karl Mannheim and the Education of an Elite', Unpublished MA dissertation, University of London.

—   (1964), 'The Elite Concept in Karl Mannheim's Sociology of Education', *Sociological Review*, 12:55-71.

Kettler, D. and Meja, V. (1995), *Karl Mannheim and the Crisis of Liberalism: The Secret of these New Times*, New Brunswick, Transaction Publishers.

Kettler, D., Meja, V. and Stehr, N. (1984), *Karl Mannheim*, Chichester, Ellis Horwood Limited.

Kudomi, Y. (1996), 'Karl Mannheim in Britain: An Interim Research Report', *Hitotsubashi Journal of Social Studies*, 28(2):43-56.

Ladwig, J. (1994), 'For whom this reform? Outlining educational policy as a social field', *British Journal of Sociology of Education*, 15(3):341-363.

Lander, G. (1983), 'Corporatist Ideologies and Education: The Case of the Business Education Council'. Unpublished PhD Thesis, University of London.

Lash, S. (1990), *Sociology of postmodernism*, London, Routledge.

Lauder, H., Hughes, D., Waslander, S., Thrupp, M., McGlinn, J., Newton, S. and Dupuis, A. (1994), *The Creation of Market Competition for Education in New Zealand*, Smithfield Project, Wellington, Victoria University of Wellington.

Lawton, D. (1975), *Class, Culture and the Curriculum*, London, Routledge.

Le Grand, J. and Bartlett, W. (eds), (1993), *Quasi-Markets and Social Policy*, London, Macmillan.

Loader, C. (1985), *The Intellectual Development of Karl Mannheim*, Cambridge, Cambridge University Press.

Mannheim, K. (1936), *Ideology and Utopia: An Introduction to the Sociology of Knowledge*, London, Kegan Paul.

— (1940), *Man and Society in an Age of Reconstruction*, London, Kegan Paul.

— (1943), *Diagnosis of Our Time: Wartime Essays of a Sociologist*, London, Kegan Paul.

— (1951), *Freedom, Power and Democratic Planning*, London, Routledge and Kegan Paul.

— (1957), *Systematic Sociology: An Introduction to the Study of Society*, (ed) J. S. Erös and W. A. C. Stewart, London, Routledge and Kegan Paul.

Mannheim, K. and Stewart, W. A. C. (1962), *An Introduction to the Sociology of Education*, London, Routledge and Kegan Paul.

Meja, V. and Kettler, D. (1993), Introduction to K. H. Wolff (ed.), *From Karl Mannheim*, New Brunswick, Transaction Publishers.

Mills, C. W. (1961), *The Sociological Imagination*, Harmondsworth, Penguin.

Moe, T. (1994), 'The British Battle for Choice' in Billingsley, K. L. (ed.), *Voices on Choice: The Education Reform Debate*, San Francisco, Pacific Institute for Public Policy.

Mortimore, P. and Goldstein, H. (1996), *The Teaching of Reading in 45 Inner London Primary Schools: a critical examination of OFSTED research,* London, Institute of Education.

Mouffe, C. (1989), 'Toward a radical democratic citizenship'. *Democratic Left,* 17(2).

Ozga, J. (1990), 'Policy Research and Policy Theory', *Journal of Education Policy,* 5(4):359-362.

Pollard, S. (1995), *Schools, Selection and the Left,* London, Social Market Foundation.

Phillips, M. (1996), 'Inspectors only come under fire when they say schools are doing badly.' *Observer,* 27 October.

Rutter, M. et al (1979), *Fifteen Thousand Hours,* London, Open Books.

Shilling, C. (1993), 'The Demise of Sociology of Education in Britain?', *British Journal of Sociology of Education,* 14(1):105-112.

Simon, B. (1994), *The State and Educational Change*, London, Lawrence and Wishart.

Smith, K. B. and Meier, K. J. (1995), *The Case Against School Choice: Politics, Markets and Fools*, Armonk, NY, M E Sharpe.

Smith, T. and Noble, M. (1995), *Education Divides: Poverty and Schooling in the 1990s*, London, Child Poverty Action Group.

Stewart, W. A. C. (1967), *Karl Mannheim on Education and Social Thought*, London, George G Harrap for the University of London Institute of Education.

Taylor, W. (1996), 'Education and the Moot' in R. Aldrich (ed.), *In History and in Education*, London, Woburn Press.

Tooley, J. (1995), 'Markets or Democracy? A Reply to Stewart Ranson', *British Journal of Educational Studies*, 43(1):21-34.

Wells, A. S. (1993a), *Time to Choose: America at the Crossroads of School Choice Policy*, New York, Hill and Wang.

— (1993b), 'The Sociology of School Choice: Why some win and others lose in the educational marketplace' in E. Rasell and R. Rothstein (eds), *School Choice: Examining the Evidence*, Washington, DC, Economic Policy Institute.

Whitty, G. (1985), *Sociology and School Knowledge: Curriculum Theory, Research and Politics,* London, Methuen.

— (1997), 'Creating Quasi-Markets in Education: A Review of Recent Research on Parental Choice and school Autonomy in Three Countries', *Review of Research in Education*, 22:3-47.

Whitty, G., Rowe, G. and Aggleton, P. (1994), 'Discourse in Cross-Curricular Contexts: Limits to Empowerment', *International Studies in Sociology of Education*, 4(1):25-42.

Whitty, G., Power, S. and Halpin, D. (1997, in press), *Devolution and Choice in Education: The School, the State and the Market*, Buckingham, Open University Press.

Woldring, H. E. S. (1986), *Karl Mannheim: The Development of his Thought*, Assen/Maastricht, Van Gorcum.

Wright, E. O. (1995), 'The Real Utopias Project', Preface to J. Cohen and J. Rogers *Associations and Democracy*, London, Verso.

Young, M. F. D. (1973), 'Taking sides against the probable', *Educational Review*, 25(3):210-222.

Young, M. and Whitty, G. (eds), (1977), *Society, State and Schooling*, Lewes, Falmer Press.